# Christmas Cakes and Cookies

**imagine** THAT!™

Imagine That! is an imprint of Top That! Publishing plc,
Tide Mill Way, Woodbridge, Suffolk, IP12 IAP, UK
www.topthatpublishing.com

# Contents

# Cooking Equipment

Before you begin to get creative in the kitchen, it's a good idea to take a look through the drawers and cupboards to make sure you know where all the cooking equipment is kept.

• To complete the recipes in this book, you will need to use a selection of everyday cooking equipment and utensils, such as mixing bowls, saucepans, a sieve, a wire rack, paper towels, knives, spoons and forks and a chopping board.

• Of course, you'll need to weigh and measure the ingredients, so you'll need a measuring jug and some kitchen scales too.

• Some of the recipes tell you to use a whisk. Ask an adult to help you use an electric whisk, or you can use a balloon whisk yourself – you'll just have to work extra hard!

• To make some of the cakes, cookies and sweets, you'll need to use the correct-sized cake tins or other special equipment. These items (and others that you may not have to hand) are listed at the start of each recipe.

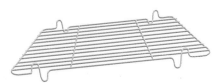

# Safety and Hygiene

It is important to take care in the kitchen as there are lots of potential hazards and hygiene risks.

- **Take Note! Whenever you see the warning triangle you will need adult supervision.**

- Before starting any cooking always wash your hands.

- Cover any cuts with a plaster.

- Wear an apron to protect your clothes.

- Always make sure that all the equipment you use is clean.

- If you need to use a sharp knife to cut up something hard, ask an adult to help you. Always use a chopping board.

- Remember that trays in the oven and pans on the cooker can get very hot. **Always ask an adult to turn on the oven and to get things in and out of the oven for you.**

- Always ask an adult for help if you are using anything electrical – like an electric whisk.

- Be careful when heating anything in a pan on top of the cooker. Keep the handle turned to one side to avoid accidentally knocking the pan.

- Keep your pets out of the kitchen while cooking.

# Getting Started

Making your own cakes and cookies is great fun and really quite easy. Best of all, everyone will enjoy what you create!

## Measuring:

Use scales to weigh exactly how much of each ingredient you need or use a measuring jug to measure liquids.

## Mixing:

Use a spoon, balloon whisk or electric hand whisk to mix the ingredients together.

## Different ideas:

Decorate your cakes and cookies with flavoured or coloured icing, and then add chocolate drops, sweets or sugar strands.

## Different shapes:

Cookie cutters come in lots of different shapes and sizes, and can be bought from most supermarkets. If you don't have any cookie cutters of your own, carefully use a knife to cut out the shapes you want.

## Creating recipes:

Once you've made a recipe in this book a few times, think about whether you could make your own version. Why not mix some chocolate chips into the Yuletide Flapjacks mixture or add desiccated coconut to the Christmas Crunchers? This way you can start to make up your own recipes and write them at the back of this book. Try to think up names for the things you create!

Read through each recipe to make sure you've got all the ingredients that you need before you start.

Always ask an adult for help if you are not sure about anything.

# Christmas Tree Cookies

These clever cookies will make your Christmas tree look really special

# Christmas Tree Cookies

**You will need:**

Extra equipment:
a baking tray
cling film
a rolling pin
a clean plastic bag
a skewer
cookie cutters
several metres of fine ribbon
or silver thread

**Ingredients:**
225 g (8 oz) plain flour
½ teaspoon ground mixed spice
100 g (4 oz) butter
100 g (4 oz) caster sugar
1 tablespoon milk
10 coloured boiled sweets

Preheat the oven to 180°C / 350°F / gas mark 4

**1** Use a paper towel to grease the baking tray with a little butter. Sift the flour and ground mixed spice into a bowl.

**2** Cut the butter into small pieces. Add it to the flour, and rub the mixture through your fingertips until it looks crumbly.

**3** Add the sugar and milk to the bowl, and knead the mixture into a soft dough. Wrap the dough in cling film and put it in the fridge for 15 minutes.

**4** Put the dough onto a floured surface and roll it out. Use cookie cutters to cut out different shapes, and put them on the baking tray.

**5** Put the boiled sweets in a plastic bag and crush them with a rolling pin. Carefully cut out a small hole from the centre of each cookie. Fill the holes with the crushed sweets. Use the skewer to pierce a hole in the top of each cookie.

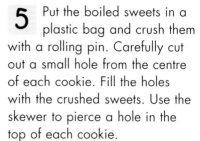

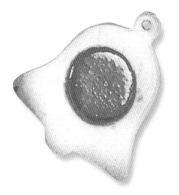

**6** Bake the cookies for 10–15 minutes, until they are golden brown and the sweets have melted. Once the melted sweets have set, carefully lift the cookies onto a wire rack to cool.

**7** Thread the hole at the top of each cookie with ribbon or thread, and hang them on your Christmas tree!

# Snowball Cupcakes

These cupcakes are so tiny you can eat loads!

# Snowball Cupcakes

You will need:

Extra equipment:
paper cases

Ingredients:
225 g (8 oz) white chocolate
25 g (1 oz) butter
225 g (8 oz) chunky fruit
and nut muesli

**1** Ask an adult to put a heatproof bowl over a saucepan of just simmering water. Make sure the bowl doesn't touch the water. Break the chocolate into small pieces and put it into the bowl with the butter. Ask an adult to help you stir the ingredients gently over a low heat until they have melted.

**Top Tip**
These little cupcakes taste just as good made with milk chocolate!

**2** Take the pan off the heat, and take the bowl off the pan. Add the muesli to the bowl and stir it into the chocolate mixture until it is thoroughly coated.

**3** Spoon a little of the mixture into each paper case. Leave the Snowball Cupcakes in a cool place to set.

11

# Christmas Truffles

A box of these chocolate truffles makes the perfect present

# Christmas Truffles

**1** Ask an adult to put a heatproof bowl over a saucepan of just-simmering water. Make sure the bowl doesn't touch the water. Break the chocolate into small pieces and put them into the bowl, and then add the cream and butter. Stir the mixture until the chocolate has melted.

You will need:
Extra equipment:
paper cases
a plastic container

Ingredients:
150 g (6 oz) plain chocolate
150 ml (5 fl oz) double cream
25 g (1 oz) butter

To coat the truffles:
cocoa powder
chocolate strands
desiccated coconut

**Top Tip**
You'll have to roll the truffle balls quickly or the mixture will literally melt in your hands!

**2** Take the saucepan off the heat. Take the bowl off the saucepan and leave it to cool for a few minutes. Carefully pour the melted chocolate into the container. Put the lid on the container and leave it in the fridge to set for 3–4 hours.

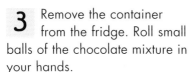

**3** Remove the container from the fridge. Roll small balls of the chocolate mixture in your hands.

**4** Roll the chocolate truffles in cocoa, chocolate strands or desiccated coconut, and then put them into the paper cases. Store the truffles in a container in the fridge until you're ready to eat them or give them as a gift.

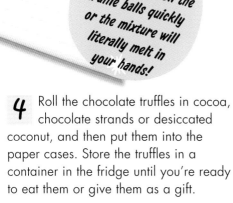

# White Festive Fudge

A wonderful treat for anyone who loves white chocolate!

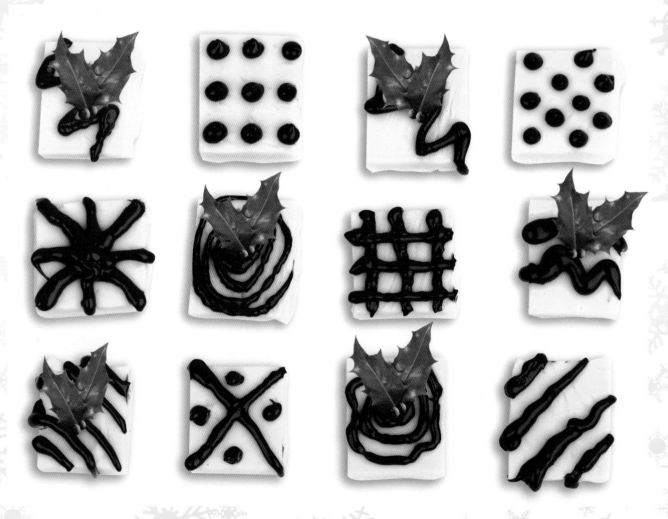

# White Festive Fudge

**1** Line the tin with greaseproof paper. Ask an adult to help you put the chocolate, vanilla essence and condensed milk into a saucepan over a medium heat. Stir them together until the chocolate has melted.

**You will need:**

**Extra equipment:**
a square baking tin 15 cm (6 in.)
greaseproof paper
an icing syringe
paper cases

**Ingredients:**
300 g (10 oz) white chocolate
200 ml (7 fl oz) sweetened condensed milk
2 teaspoons vanilla essence

**To decorate:**
50 g (2 oz) plain chocolate
holly leaf decorations

**2** Ask an adult to pour the mixture into the tin, and smooth the top with the back of a metal spoon. Put the tin into the fridge for 3–4 hours.

**3** Remove the fudge from the tin by lifting it with the greaseproof paper. Turn it out onto a board and peel off the paper. Cut the slab of fudge into squares.

**4** Ask an adult to put a heatproof bowl over a saucepan of just-simmering water. Make sure the bowl doesn't touch the water. Break the chocolate into the bowl, and stir until it has melted. Put the melted chocolate into an icing syringe and decorate the squares of fudge. When the chocolate has set, put the pieces of fudge into paper cases. Lay a few festive holly leaves on top to finish.

# Snowflake Delight

This Turkish delight is sweet and juicy to eat!

# Snowflake Delight

**You will need:**
Extra equipment:
a small square dish

Ingredients:
a packet of jelly,
any flavour you like

To decorate:
icing sugar or
desiccated coconut

**1** Cut the jelly into cubes and put it into a heatproof jug. Ask an adult to prepare the jelly following the packet instructions. Stir the jelly with a wooden spoon until it has dissolved. Pour the jelly into the dish and put it in the fridge to set.

**Top Tip**
Try pouring a little melted chocolate on top for an even better taste!

**2** When the jelly has set, loosen the edges from the dish and cut it into squares.

**3** Carefully turn the jelly out onto a plate or board covered in icing sugar or coconut. Turn the squares of jelly until they are completely covered.

# Easy Christmas Cake

### Make this festive treat for your whole family to enjoy

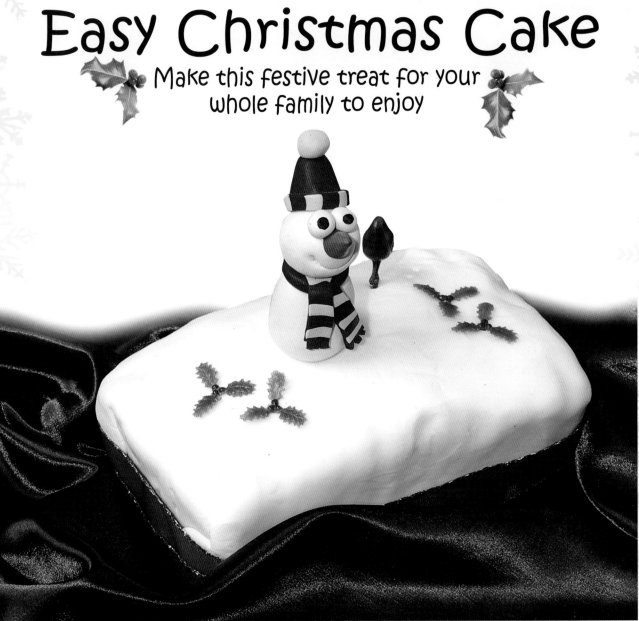

# Easy Christmas Cake

You will need:

Extra equipment:
a loaf tin 20 x 13 cm (8 x 5 in.)

Ingredients:
100 g (4 oz) margarine
1 large egg
1 tablespoon pear and apple spread
or thick honey
150 g (6 oz) self-raising
wholemeal flour
225 g (8 oz) mincemeat
orange juice

To decorate:
100 g (4 oz) icing sugar
1-2 tablespoons orange juice

Preheat the oven to 160°C / 325°F /
gas mark 3

**Top Tip**
Tie a wide ribbon around your cake and add festive decorations.

**1** Grease the loaf tin with a little margarine. Put the margarine, egg and pear and apple spread (or honey) in a bowl and mix them together until they're light and creamy.

**2** Sift the flour into the bowl, and mix it in gently. Add the mincemeat and mix well. Then add enough orange juice to make a soft mixture.

**3** Put the mixture into the tin, smoothing the top with the spoon. Bake for 40 minutes, until it is golden brown.

**4** Leave the cake in the tin for five minutes, and then turn it out onto a wire rack to cool.

**5** Sieve the icing sugar into a bowl, and mix in enough orange juice to make a thick paste. Spoon the mixture over the cake, letting it run down the sides.

19

# Gingerbread Reindeer

Don't stop at Rudolph – make all his friends too!

# Gingerbread Reindeer

**1** Put the sugar, syrup, treacle, cinnamon, ginger, ground cloves and a tiny bit of water into a pan.

You will need:

**Extra equipment:**
greaseproof paper, cling film
a reindeer-shaped cookie cutter or knife
a baking tray

**Ingredients:**
75 g (2½ oz) soft brown sugar
2 tablespoons golden syrup
1 tablespoon black treacle
1 teaspoon cinnamon
1 teaspoon ginger
1 teaspoon ground cloves
100 g (3½ oz) butter, softened
½ teaspoon bicarbonate of soda
225 g (8 oz) plain flour

**To decorate:**
50 g (2 oz) icing sugar
1 tablespoon orange juice
food colouring

**Preheat the oven to**
180°C / 350°F / gas mark 4

**2** Ask an adult to heat up the mixture, stirring all the time with a wooden spoon, until it is bubbling hard.

**3** Turn off the heat, then stir in the butter, bicarbonate of soda and flour until you have a smooth dough.

21

**4** Wrap the dough in a piece of cling film and leave it in the fridge for 30 minutes.

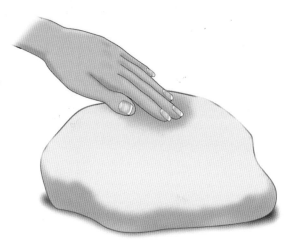

**5** Place the dough onto a sheet of greaseproof paper, then put another sheet on top. Using a rolling pin, roll the dough flat between the sheets until it is 3 mm ($\frac{1}{8}$ inch) thick.

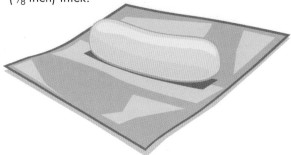

**7** Bake the cookies for 15 to 20 minutes, until they are firm. Ask an adult to remove the hot tray from the oven. Use a spatula to transfer the cookies to a wire rack to cool. Once cool, decorate with icing (see page 41), adding a few drops of food colouring if you want to.

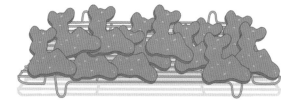

**6** Using a reindeer-shaped cookie cutter or a sharp knife, cut out cookies from the flat dough. Place the shapes onto a baking tray covered with a sheet of greaseproof paper.

**8** For a little bit of extra fun you could cover the reindeer with melted chocolate and add a red sweet for his nose.

# Snowball Cakes

These snowballs are much too tasty for throwing!

# Snowball Cakes

**Take Note!**
Ask an adult to help you use the electric whisk.

**You will need:**

Extra equipment:
a baking tray
greaseproof paper
paper cases

Ingredients:
75 g (2 1/2 oz) icing sugar
225 g (8 oz) butter, softened
2 teaspoons vanilla essence
250 g (9 oz) plain flour
90 g (3 oz) nuts, pecans or almonds finely chopped
1/2 teaspoon salt

To decorate:
icing sugar

Preheat the oven to 170°C / 325°F / gas mark 3

**1** With a wooden spoon or electric whisk, mix the icing sugar, butter and vanilla essence together in a mixing bowl until you have a smooth paste.

**2** Add the flour, nuts and salt to the mixture and stir. Keep mixing until all the ingredients are combined and you have a smooth dough.

**3** Using a teaspoon, spoon dollops of the dough onto a baking tray lined with greaseproof paper.

**4** Bake the Snowball Cakes for 15 to 20 minutes. They should be just golden, so make sure you don't overcook them!

**5** Ask an adult to remove the hot tray from the oven. Roll the Snowball Cakes across a plate of icing sugar before they cool completely.

**6** Leave the decorated Snowball Cakes on a wire rack to cool. Serve them in paper cases with an extra dusting of icing sugar for a really snowy finish!

# Shortbread Snowmen

The sugar on these crunchy snowmen glistens like frost!

# Shortbread Snowmen

**1** Put the butter and sugar into a mixing bowl. Using a wooden spoon, mix them together until they make a smooth paste.

You will need:

Extra equipment:
greaseproof paper
a snowman-shaped cookie cutter or a sharp knife
a baking tray
a rolling pin

Ingredients:
100 g (3 1/2 oz) butter, softened
60 g (2 oz) golden caster sugar
100 g (3 1/2 oz) plain flour
60 g (2 oz) fine semolina
sugar to sprinkle

Preheat the oven to 150°C / 300°F / gas mark 2

**Top Tip**
You can use melted chocolate or icing to decorate your snowmen

**2** Sift the flour into the bowl.

**3** Add the semolina and then stir the mixture well.

**4** When it seems as if the mixture won't stir any more, use your hands to knead it. The dough will be ready when it is smooth and there are no bits left on the sides of the bowl.

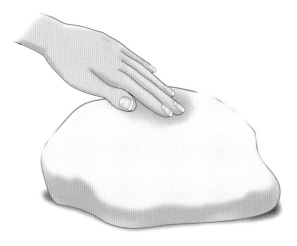

**6** Use a snowman-shaped cookie cutter or a sharp knife to cut out shapes from the dough. Lay the shapes on a baking tray lined with greaseproof paper.

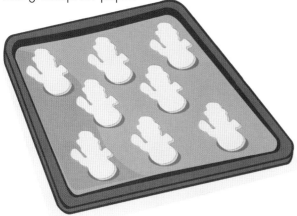

**5** Place the mixture on top of a sheet of greaseproof paper, then put another sheet on top. Using a rolling pin, roll the dough flat between the sheets until it is about 3 mm ($1/8$ inch) thick.

**7** Bake the shortbread for 17 minutes. Ask an adult to remove the hot tray from the oven. Use a spatula to lift the snowmen onto a wire rack to cool.

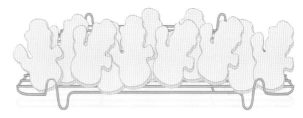

**8** Sprinkle the snowmen with sugar to make them glisten. Why not make a cool Santa shortbread and cover with coloured icing?

27

# Snowflakes

Try this simple recipe for some tasty chocolate treats!

# Snowflakes

You will need:
Extra equipment:
paper cases

Ingredients:
200 g (7 oz) white chocolate
120 g (4 oz) cornflakes

**1** Ask an adult to put a heatproof bowl over a saucepan of just-simmering water. Make sure the bowl doesn't touch the water. Break the chocolate into small pieces and put it into the bowl. Stir the ingredients gently over a low heat until they have melted.

**Top Tip**
These little cakes taste just as good made with milk chocolate!

**2** Stir the chocolate and the cornflakes together in a large mixing bowl.

**3** Spoon the mixture into individual paper cases.

**4** Leave the Snowflakes in the fridge for 2 hours, or until the chocolate has set.

29

# Hazelnut Candles

These crunchy candles look great decorated
with silver balls and sweets!

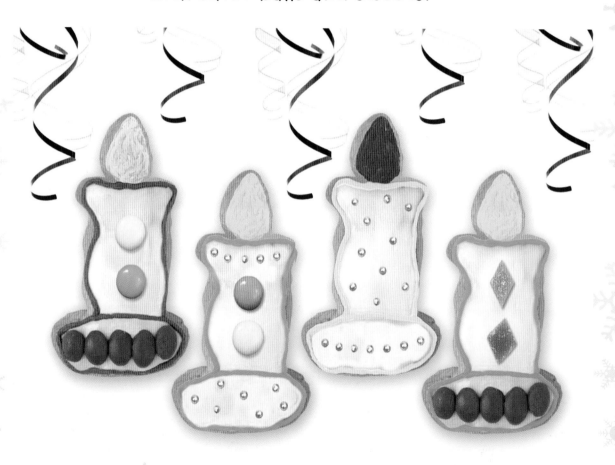

# Hazelnut Candles

**Top Tip**
To soften the butter, take it out of the fridge at least 30 minutes before cooking.

**You will need:**

Extra equipment:
greaseproof paper
a candle-shaped cookie cutter or knife
a baking tray
a rolling pin

Ingredients:
120 g (4 oz) butter, softened
120 g (4 oz) sugar
1/2 teaspoon lemon juice
1 pinch cinnamon
1 pinch ground cloves
1 pinch nutmeg
230 g (8 oz) plain flour
100 g (3 1/2 oz) hazelnuts, ground
75 g (2 1/2 oz) icing sugar
1 tablespoon water

Preheat the oven to 200°C / 400°F / gas mark 6

**1** Mix the butter, sugar, lemon juice, cinnamon, ground cloves, nutmeg, flour and hazelnuts together in a bowl with a wooden spoon until a smooth dough is made.

**2** Place the mixture on top of a sheet of greaseproof paper, then put another sheet on top. Using a rolling pin, roll the dough flat between the sheets until it is 6 mm (1/4 inch) thick.

**3** Using a candle-shaped cookie cutter or a sharp knife, cut out cookies from the dough. Place them onto a baking tray lined with greaseproof paper.

**4** Bake the cookies for 12 minutes, or until they are golden brown. Ask an adult to take the hot tray from the oven. Use a spatula to transfer the cookies to a wire rack to cool.

**5** Why not ice your Hazelnut Candles with a delicious sugar coating? Find out how to make icing on page 41. You could decorate your cookies with pretty silver balls and sweets if you like!

# Christmas Macaroons

 Perfect while you wait for Christmas dinner!

# Christmas Macaroons

**Take Note!**
Ask an adult to help you use the electric whisk.

**You will need:**

Extra equipment:
a baking tray
greaseproof paper

Ingredients:
2 egg whites
1/2 teaspoon lemon juice
a pinch of salt
150 g (5 oz) icing sugar
1/2 teaspoon cinnamon
150 g (5 oz) desiccated coconut

Preheat the oven to 150°C / 300°F / gas mark 2

**1** Whisk the egg whites in a mixing bowl until they form soft peaks.

**2** Carry on whisking while adding the lemon juice, salt, icing sugar and cinnamon a little at a time. Be careful not to whisk too much, though, or the mixture will go soft. Now fold in the coconut.

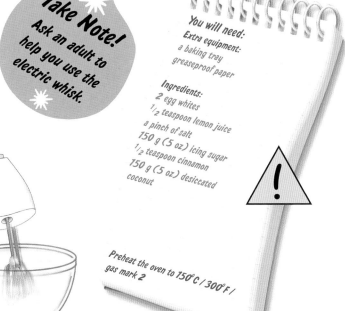

**3** Using a tablespoon, scoop dollops of the mixture onto a baking tray lined with greaseproof paper. Make sure you leave spaces between the dollops as they will expand during cooking!

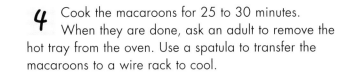

**4** Cook the macaroons for 25 to 30 minutes. When they are done, ask an adult to remove the hot tray from the oven. Use a spatula to transfer the macaroons to a wire rack to cool.

# Yuletide Log

## This cake makes a perfect teatime treat

# Yuletide Log

**1** Put the tin on a sheet of greaseproof paper and draw around it, leaving an edge of 2.5 cm (1 in.). Cut out the paper shape, and make a slit at each corner. Grease the tin with some soft margarine. Now fit the paper into the tin, folding in the edges. Finally, grease the paper.

You will need:
Extra equipment:
a swiss roll tin
22.5 x 30 cm
(9 x 12 in.)
greaseproof paper

Ingredients:
3 large eggs
margarine to grease
75 g (3 oz) caster sugar
75 g (3 oz) self-raising flour

For the filling and the top:
3 tablespoons of raspberry or
strawberry jam, or chocolate spread
caster sugar

Preheat the oven to 220°C / 425°F/
gas mark 7

**Take Note!** Ask an adult to help you use the electric whisk.

**2** Break the eggs into a large bowl. Add the sugar, and whisk for a few minutes until the mixture is very light and creamy.

**4** Put the mixture into the tin, and then smooth the top with the back of a tablespoon. Bake for 7–10 minutes, until the edges have shrunk slightly away from the tin. Leave the cake to cool in the tin for 1–2 minutes.

**3** Hold the sieve above the bowl and sift the flour into the mixture. Use a tablespoon to stir in the flour, using a gentle figure-of-eight movement – you don't want to knock out the air you've just whisked in!

35

**5** Lay out another sheet of greaseproof paper and sprinkle caster sugar all over it. While the cake is still warm, turn it out onto the paper. Trim off the edges with a knife.

**6** Spread the cake with jam or chocolate spread. Now roll the cake quite tightly, using the greaseproof paper to help you. Sprinkle some caster sugar over the cake to finish.

*Top Tip*
*Stand the jar of jam or chocolate spread in hot water for about 10 minutes before you need to use it. This will make it easier to spread.*

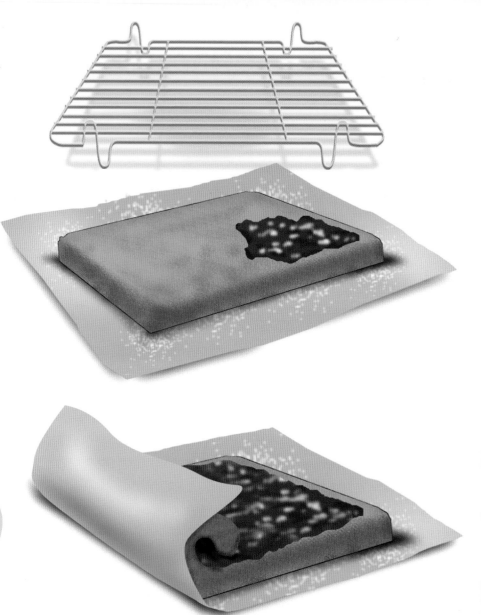

# Winter Snow Cupcakes

These cupcakes are ice-cool!

# Winter Snow Cupcakes

**1** Put the paper cases in the bun tin.

You will need:
Extra equipment:
a bun tin
paper cases

Ingredients:
3 eggs
150 g (5 oz) butter, softened
150 g (5 oz) sugar
175 g (6 oz) self-raising flour
1 teaspoon vanilla essence

For the topping:
ready-to-roll fondant icing
blue food colouring

Preheat the oven to 175°C / 350°F / gas mark 4

**Take Note!** Ask an adult to help you use the electric whisk.

**2** Crack the eggs into a bowl and beat lightly with a fork. Add the beaten eggs to a large bowl containing the butter, sugar, flour and vanilla essence.

**3** Beat with an electric mixer for 2 minutes, until the mixture is light and creamy.

**4** Use a teaspoon to transfer equal amounts of the mixture to the paper cases. Bake the cupcakes for 18–20 minutes. Leave them to cool on a wire rack.

**5** Knead a couple of drops of food colouring into half the fondant icing. When the colour is even, roll out the icing and cut out snowflake shapes to cover each cupcake. Decorate with small white icing snowflakes.

# Christmas Party Cakes

Use lots of brightly coloured icing to decorate these brilliant cakes!

# Christmas Party Cakes

You will need:

Extra equipment:
paper cases
a bun tin
an icing syringe (optional)

Ingredients:
225 g (8 oz) self-raising flour
75 g (3 oz) margarine
75 g (3 oz) caster sugar
1 egg
75-100 ml (3-4 fl oz) milk

Turn to the next page to find out how to make different-flavoured cakes.

Preheat the oven to 200°C / 400°F/ gas mark 6

**1** Put the paper cases in the bun tin. Sift the flour into a bowl.

**2** Put the margarine in the bowl. Use the tips of your fingers to rub the margarine and flour together until the mixture becomes crumbly.

**3** Add the sugar and mix it in. Now stir in the egg. Finally, add enough milk to make the mixture creamy.

**4** Put spoonfuls of the mixture into the paper cases. Bake the cakes for 10–15 minutes, until they are golden brown, then leave them to cool on a wire rack.

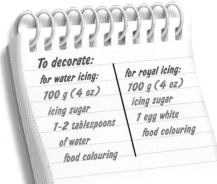

To decorate:

| for water icing: | for royal icing: |
|---|---|
| 100 g (4 oz) icing sugar | 100 g (4 oz) icing sugar |
| 1-2 tablespoons of water | 1 egg white |
| food colouring | food colouring |

# Decorating the Christmas Party Cakes

**1** Cover the cakes with water icing. Here's how to make it! Sift the icing sugar into a bowl. Add 1–2 tablespoons of hot water and mix until you have a smooth thick paste. Add one or two drops of food colouring if you want coloured icing.

To make chocolate icing, add one teaspoon of cocoa powder to the icing sugar before sifting. To make lemon icing, add 1–2 tablespoons of lemon juice instead of hot water.

You can decorate your cakes with sugar sprinkles, silver balls or sweets. Once the water icing has set, why not pipe decorations with royal icing?

**2** To make royal icing, beat an egg white in a small bowl. Sift the icing sugar into the bowl. Beat the mixture until the icing becomes smooth and thick. Add a drop of food colouring if you wish. Spoon the icing into an icing syringe and carefully pipe your decoration onto the cakes. Leave the icing to set.

**Top Tip**
Decorate your cakes with sugared diamonds, sugar sprinkles, silver balls or small sweets!

# Variations

## Chocolate Chip Party Cakes

Sift 25 g (1 oz) cocoa into the bowl with the flour. Mix in a handful of chocolate chips. When the cakes are cooked and cooled, cover them with chocolate water icing (see method above).

## Coconut Party Cakes

Add 50 g (2 oz) desiccated coconut to the mixture with the sugar. When the cakes are cooked, top them with lemon water icing (see method above) and sprinkle them with more coconut.

## Cherry Party Cakes

Add 100 g (4 oz) chopped glacé cherries to the mixture with the sugar. When the cakes are cooked, cover them with lemon water icing (see method above) and top each cake with half a glacé cherry.

41

# Angel Cakes

These cakes may look fancy, but they're simple to make!

# Angel Cakes

**1** Put the paper cases in the bun tin.

You will need:
Extra equipment:
a bun tin
paper cases

Ingredients:
100 g (4 oz) butter, softened
100 g (4 oz) granulated sugar
2 eggs
100 g (4 oz) self-raising flour

For the buttercream icing:
75 g (3 oz) butter
150 g (6 oz) icing sugar
1-2 tablespoons milk
food colouring (optional)

Preheat the oven to 190°C / 375°F /
gas mark 5

**Top Tip**
To soften the butter, take it out of the fridge at least 30 minutes before cooking.

**2** Put the butter and sugar into a mixing bowl. Use a wooden spoon to beat them together until the mixture is fluffy and very pale in colour.

**4** Sift the rest of the flour into the bowl. Use a tablespoon to mix the ingredients gently, as if you were drawing a figure-of-eight. This will make sure your mixture stays nice and fluffy.

**5** Use a teaspoon to transfer equal amounts of the mixture to the paper cases. Bake the cakes for 20–25 minutes or until they are well risen and golden brown. Leave them to cool on a wire rack.

**3** Beat in the eggs, one at a time, adding a tablespoon of flour with each one.

# Cranberry Orange Muffins

## Munch these tasty muffins as a snack with a drink

# Cranberry Orange Muffins

**You will need:**

Extra equipment:
a muffin tray
paper cases

Ingredients:
250 g (9 oz) plain flour
150 g (5 oz) sugar
1 tablespoon baking powder
1 egg
175 ml (6 fl oz) milk
3 tablespoons vegetable oil
80 g (1 oz) chopped cranberries
2 tablespoons grated orange peel
2 tablespoons chopped pecans
or walnuts

Preheat the oven to 230°C / 445°F /
gas mark 8

⚠️

**Take Note!**
Graters are sharp,
so take care to mind
your fingers!

**1** Put the paper cases in the muffin tray.

**2** Sift the flour, sugar and baking powder into a bowl. Mix them together.

**4** Fold in the cranberries, orange peel and nuts.

**3** Add in the egg, milk and vegetable oil and mix until all the flour is moistened.

**5** Use a teaspoon to transfer equal amounts of the mixture to the paper cases. Bake the muffins for 20 minutes or until they are well risen and golden brown. Leave them to cool on a wire rack.

# Christmas Spice Muffins

 Put a little spice into christmas

# Christmas Spice Muffins

**1** Use a paper towel to grease the muffin tray with a little soft butter.

You will need:
Extra equipment:
a muffin tray

Ingredients:
110 g (4 oz) butter
135 g (5 oz) sugar
2 eggs
½ teaspoon ground cinnamon
½ teaspoon ground allspice
2 teaspoons baking powder
½ teaspoon bicarbonate of soda
235 ml (8 fl oz) apple sauce
190 g (7 oz) plain flour
For the topping:
2 tablespoons water
120 g (4 oz) icing sugar
nuts of your choice

Preheat the oven to 180°C / 355°F / gas mark 4

**2** In a large bowl mix together the butter and sugar until the mixture is creamy.

**3** Add in the eggs and beat until smooth. Blend in the cinnamon, allspice, baking powder and bicarbonate of soda.

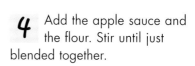

**4** Add the apple sauce and the flour. Stir until just blended together.

**5** Use a teaspoon to divide the mixture equally into the muffin tray. Bake the muffins for 20 minutes.

**6** When the muffins are cool, mix the icing sugar and water and spoon a little icing over each one. Top with a few nuts.

# Happy New Year Cake

Start the new year with this 'marble-ous' cake!

# Happy New Year Cake

**1** Put the cake tin onto a sheet of greaseproof paper and draw around it. Cut out the circle of paper. Use a paper towel to grease the tin with a little soft margarine, and then put the circle of greaseproof paper inside the tin. Grease the paper.

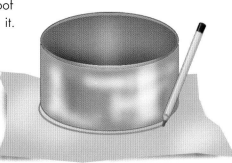

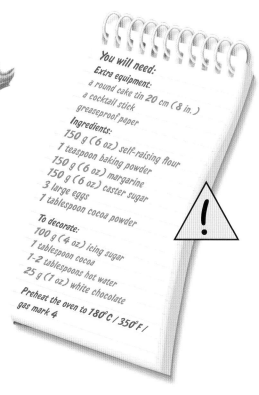

You will need:
Extra equipment:
a round cake tin 20 cm (8 in.)
a cocktail stick
greaseproof paper

Ingredients:
150 g (6 oz) self-raising flour
1 teaspoon baking powder
150 g (6 oz) margarine
150 g (6 oz) caster sugar
3 large eggs
1 tablespoon cocoa powder

To decorate:
100 g (4 oz) icing sugar
1 tablespoon cocoa
1-2 tablespoons hot water
25 g (1 oz) white chocolate

Preheat the oven to 180°C / 350°F / gas mark 4

**2** Sift the flower and baking powder into a mixing bowl.

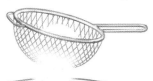

**3** Add the margarine, sugar and eggs. Beat everything together with a wooden spoon until completely mixed.

**4** Put half the mixture into another bowl, and then sift the cocoa on top of it. Mix it in well.

49

**5** Put alternate spoonfuls of the different-coloured mixtures into the tin. Swirl them together a little, and then smooth the top. Put the tin in the centre of the oven and bake for 40–50 minutes.

**6** Take the cake out of the oven and leave it in the tin for five minutes. Turn it out onto a wire rack, peel off the greaseproof paper, turn it over and leave it to cool.

# Decorating the Cake

**1** Before you start to decorate the cake, ask an adult to help you cut it in half as shown.

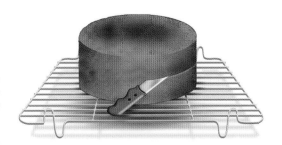

**2** Sift the icing sugar and cocoa into a bowl. Add the hot water, and stir the ingredients together until the mixture is completely chocolate brown.

**3** Spread some icing on the one half of the cake, and then place the other half on top to sandwich the icing. Pour the rest of the icing over the top of the cake and neatly spread it to the edges.

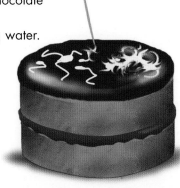

**4** Melt the white chocolate in a bowl over a saucepan of simmering water. (Make sure the bowl doesn't touch the water.) Spoon blobs of white chocolate onto the cake, and use a cocktail stick to make the marble effect shown.

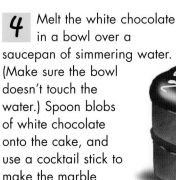

# Christmas Crunchers

Leave one for Santa and listen out for the crunch!

# Christmas Crunchers

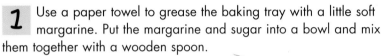

You will need:
Extra equipment:
a baking tray
a round cookie cutter 5 cm (2 in.)

Ingredients:
100 g (4 oz) soft margarine
75 g (3 oz) demerara sugar
100 g (4 oz) plain wholemeal flour
100 g (4 oz) porridge oats

Preheat the oven to 180°C / 350°F / gas mark 4

**1** Use a paper towel to grease the baking tray with a little soft margarine. Put the margarine and sugar into a bowl and mix them together with a wooden spoon.

**2** Add the flour and the oats to the bowl. Mix everything together, using a spoon and then your hands, to make a soft dough.

**3** Put the dough onto a floured surface and gently press it out.

**4** Cut out circles of dough and put them onto the baking tray.

**5** Bake the crunchers in the oven for 12–15 minutes, until they are golden brown. Place the cookies onto a wire rack to cool.

# Peppermint Creams

Coat these icy mints with chocolate for a cool christmas kick!

# Peppermint Creams

**1** Sift the icing sugar into a bowl.

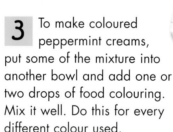

**2** Whisk the egg white in a bowl until it's frothy, then add it to the icing sugar with a few drops of peppermint essence. Mix it together with the wooden spoon to make a very thick paste. Knead the paste with your hands until it is very smooth.

**3** To make coloured peppermint creams, put some of the mixture into another bowl and add one or two drops of food colouring. Mix it well. Do this for every different colour used.

You will need:
Extra equipment:
none

Ingredients:
450 g (1 lb) icing sugar
1 egg white
a few drops of peppermint essence
food colouring (optional)

For chocolate peppermint creams:
100 g (4 oz) plain chocolate, melted

**Top Tip**
Use food colouring to make different-coloured peppermint creams.

**4** Use your hands to make small balls of paste and flatten them into discs. Put them onto a wire rack to harden slightly.

**5** You could dip your peppermint creams into melted chocolate. Leave them to set on the wire rack.

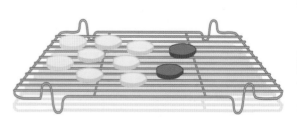

# Carrot Muffins

Rudolph loves these muffins – they help him see in the dark!

# Carrot Muffins

**1** Use a paper towel to grease the muffin tray with a little soft butter.

You will need:
Extra equipment:
a muffin tray

Ingredients:
125 g (4 ½ oz) wholemeal flour
125 g (4 ½ oz) plain flour
100 g (4 oz) raisins
60 g (2 oz) brown sugar
1 teaspoon baking powder
225 ml (8 fl oz) milk
100 g (4 oz) shredded carrot
2 eggs
55 g (2 oz) butter, melted

Preheat the oven to 190°C / 375°F / gas mark 5

**2** In a large bowl put the wholemeal flour, plain flour, raisins, sugar and baking powder. Stir them all together with a wooden spoon until they are well mixed.

**3** Put the remaining ingredients in a small bowl and mix together. Then add to the larger bowl and mix together.

**4** Use a teaspoon to divide the mixture equally into the muffin tray. Bake the muffins for 20 minutes.

**5** Leave the muffins in the tray until they are cool, and then turn out and enjoy.

# Wild Berry Muffins

Your friends will go wild for these fruity Christmas treats!

# Wild Berry Muffins

**1** Use a paper towel to grease the muffin tray with a little soft butter.

You will need:
Extra equipment:
a muffin tray

Ingredients:
250 g (9 oz) plain flour
150 g (5 oz) sugar
2 ½ teaspoons baking powder
¼ teaspoon bicarbonate of soda
240 ml (8 fl oz) milk
115 ml (4 fl oz) vegetable oil
2 eggs
190 g (7 oz) fresh berries

Preheat the oven to 200°C / 390°F/
gas mark 6

**Take Note!** Ask an adult to help you use the electric whisk.

**2** Sift the flour, sugar, baking powder and bicarbonate of soda in a large bowl. Mix them together.

**3** In another bowl, whisk the milk, oil and eggs. Add to the dry ingredients and mix well until just blended.

**4** Fold the berries into the mixture.

**5** Use a teaspoon to divide the mixture equally into the muffin tray. Bake the muffins for 15–20 minutes or until golden brown.

**6** Loosen the edges and turn out onto a wire rack to cool.

# Christmas Muffins

## The perfect alternative to mince pies!

# Christmas Muffins

**1** Put the paper cases in the muffin tray.

**2** Put the butter, the sugar, the egg and the flour into a large mixing bowl. Stir them all together with a wooden spoon until they are well mixed.

**3** Sift the baking powder and cocoa powder into the bowl. Add the milk. Mix them together.

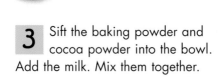

You will need:

Extra equipment:
a muffin tray
paper cases

Ingredients:
50 g (2 oz) butter, softened
75 g (3 oz) brown sugar
1 egg
100 g (4 oz) plain flour
2 teaspoons baking powder
1 tablespoon cocoa powder
90 ml (3 fl oz) milk

To decorate:
fresh cream
chocolate snowflakes

Preheat the oven to 260°C / 500°F / gas mark 10

**Top Tip**
To soften the butter, take it out of the fridge at least 30 minutes before cooking.

**4** Use a teaspoon to divide the mixture equally into the muffin tray. Bake the muffins for 12 minutes.

**5** Leave the muffins in the tray until they are cool, and then decorate them with fresh whipped cream. Add a little chocolate snowflake to finish.

# Variations for the Christmas Muffins

**1** Put the paper cases in the muffin tray. Sift the flour into a bowl.

**2** Put the margarine in the bowl. Use the tips of your fingers to rub the margarine and flour together until the mixture becomes crumbly.

**3** Add the sugar and stir in the egg. Finally, add enough milk to make the mixture creamy.

**4** Put spoonfuls of the mixture into the paper cases. Bake the muffins for 10–15 minutes, then leave them to cool on a wire rack.

**5** Decorate them with a generous swirl of fresh whipped cream. Cover with coconut and add a chocolate snowflake.

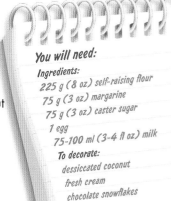

**You will need:**

Ingredients:
225 g (8 oz) self-raising flour
75 g (3 oz) margarine
75 g (3 oz) caster sugar
1 egg
75-100 ml (3-4 fl oz) milk

**To decorate:**
dessiccated coconut
fresh cream
chocolate snowflakes

# Christmas Crackle Cakes

Use cornflakes or crisped rice to make
these little cakes crackle!

# Christmas Crackle Cakes

You will need:
Extra equipment:
paper cases

Ingredients:
25 g (1 oz) sugar
25 g (1 oz) butter
2 tablespoons cocoa
1 tablespoon golden syrup or honey
25 g (1 oz) cornflakes

To decorate:
coloured chocolate drops

**Top Tip**
Use crisped rice instead of cornflakes if you prefer.

**1** Put the sugar, butter, cocoa and golden syrup or honey into a pan over a low heat. Stir until the ingredients have melted.

**2** Stir the cornflakes into the mixture until they are completely coated.

**3** Spoon a little of the mixture into each of the paper cases. Top each with a coloured chocolate drop and leave them to set.

# Yuletide Flapjacks

These yummy flapjacks are perfect to munch on long journeys when visiting friends!

# Yuletide Flapjacks

**1** Use a paper towel to grease the tin with a little butter. Put the butter, sugar and honey (or golden syrup) in a pan over a low heat. Stir the ingredients together until the butter has melted and the sugar has dissolved.

**2** Take the pan off the heat and stir in the porridge oats, mixing well. If you are making fruit and nut flapjacks, stir in these ingredients as well.

**3** Spread the mixture into the tin, and press it down with the back of a spoon. Bake the flapjacks for 20–25 minutes. Take care not to overcook them or they will taste too dry. Cut the mixture into twelve pieces, and leave them in the tin to cool completely.

You will need:

Extra equipment:
a baking tin 28 x 18 cm (11 x 7 in.)

Ingredients:
225 g (8 oz) butter
75 g (3 oz) sugar
2 tablespoons honey or golden syrup
350 g (12 oz) porridge oats

For fruit and nut flapjacks:
100 g (4 oz) sultanas, raisins or currants
50 g (2 oz) chopped nuts

For chocolate flapjacks:
100 g (4 oz) plain chocolate

Preheat the oven to 180°C / 350°F / gas mark 4

Take Note!
Ask an adult to help you melt the ingredients.

## Chocolate Flapjacks:

**1** Ask an adult to help you melt the chocolate in a heatproof bowl over a pan of simmering water.

**2** Take the bowl off the pan. Dip the ends of each flapjack into the melted chocolate, and leave them to set on a wire rack.

# Energy Bars

These spicy bars give Santa's elves all the energy they need!

# Energy Bars

**1** Lightly grease the tin with a little butter and line it with a piece of greaseproof paper.

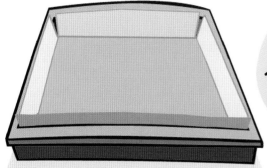

**Top Tip**
Dip the spoon in hot water before measuring out the treacle. The treacle will slip off the spoon!

**You will need:**
Extra equipment:
a square tin 18 cm (7 in.)
greaseproof paper
an icing syringe

**Ingredients:**
100 g (4 oz) butter
75 g (3 oz) caster sugar
2 eggs
2 tablespoons black treacle
100 g (4 oz) plain flour
1 ½ teaspoons baking powder
1 teaspoon ground cinnamon
1 teaspoon mixed spice
225 g (8 oz) raisins
50 g (2 oz) walnuts, chopped

Preheat the oven to 180°C / 350°F / gas mark 4

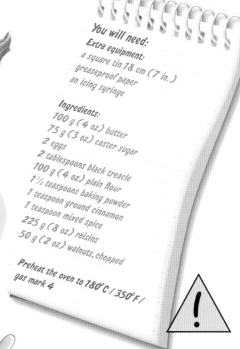

**2** Put the butter and sugar into a large bowl and beat them together until they are light and creamy.

**To decorate:**
2 tablespoons icing sugar
2 teaspoons water

**3** Beat the eggs together with a fork in a small bowl. Add them to the butter mixture, a little at a time, and mix them in well. Now mix in the treacle.

**4** Sift the flour, baking powder, cinnamon and spices into the bowl.

**5** Stir in the raisins and walnuts.

**6** Spoon the mixture into the tin and smooth the top with the back of the spoon. Bake for 15–20 minutes.

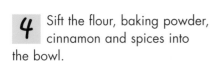
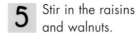

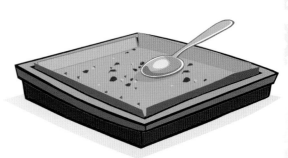

**7** Remove the tin from the oven. When it is cool enough to touch, cut twelve bars from the mixture and transfer them to a wire rack.

**8** You can ice the bars when they are completely cool. Sift the icing sugar into a bowl and add the water, mixing well with a wooden spoon to make a thick paste. Spoon the icing into the icing syringe and decorate the bars with Christmas star patterns.

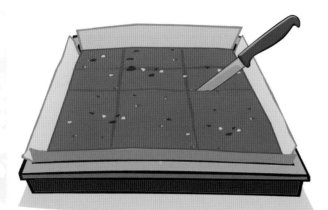

# Coconut Ice

These simple sweets can be made in any colours you like!

# Coconut Ice

**1** Put the tin on the greaseproof paper and draw around it. Cut out the square of paper large enough to overlap the sides, slit the corners and put it into the tin.

**2** Ask an adult to help you put the sugar, butter and milk into a pan over a medium heat, and bring the mixture to the boil. Let the mixture simmer for four minutes, stirring all the time.

**Top Tip**
Why not make green and white coconut ice?

**5** Colour the other half of the mixture with a few drops of food colouring. Pour it on top of the mixture in the tin and leave it to set. Cut the Coconut Ice into squares, but be careful – it will be very crumbly!

**4** Ask the adult to pour half the mixture into the tin. Leave it to cool a little.

**3** Remove the pan from the heat and stir in the coconut.

# Festive Fondue

### Share this chocolate fondue with your whole family

Most fruit is available in supermarkets all year round. There is no reason why you can't have your favourite fruit at Christmas covered in smooth chocolate.

# Festive Fondue

**1** Put the white and plain chocolate in separate heatproof bowls. Ask an adult to help you put some water in a saucepan over a medium heat, and then to place one of the bowls on top (making sure it doesn't touch the water). When the chocolate has melted, take the bowl off the pan, and replace it with the other bowl to melt the rest of the chocolate.

**You will need:**

**Extra equipment:**
cocktail sticks

**Ingredients:**
100 g (4 oz) plain chocolate
100 g (4 oz) white chocolate

**A selection of fresh fruits to dip:**
strawberries
fresh cherries
seedless grapes
mango
banana
pineapple

**Alternative dried fruits to dip:**
whole, stoned, ready-to-serve
apricots and prunes
glace cherries

**Top Tip**
Try putting chocolate-coated banana chunks in the freezer for one hour before eating – really delicious!

**2** Meanwhile, prepare the fruit. Leave the stalks on the strawberries and the cherries, and cut the mango, the pineapple and the banana into thick slices.

**3** Take it in turns to dip the fruit in the melted chocolate, holding each piece by its stalk or with the cocktail stick.

# Variation

Try this with dried fruits: whole, stoned, ready-to-serve dried apricots and prunes, and glacé cherries which can be dipped in the melted chocolate in the same way as fresh fruit.

# Santa Sweets

Make Santa's favourite sweets, they are delicious!

# Santa Sweets

**1** Put the almonds, sugar and a little orange juice in a bowl. Mix them together to form a stiff paste.

You will need:

Extra equipment:
paper cases
a cocktail stick

Ingredients:
150 g (6 oz) ground almonds
100 g (4 oz) caster sugar
1-2 tablespoons orange juice

To decorate:
icing sugar

For chocolate almond sweets:
cocoa powder or
50 g (2 oz) plain chocolate, melted

**2** Use your hands to roll the paste into small balls. To decorate, put a little icing sugar on a plate and roll the balls around in it until they are evenly coated.

**3** For chocolate almond sweets, you can either roll the balls in cocoa powder or cover them with melted chocolate. Use a cocktail stick to dip the almond sweets into the melted chocolate, and then leave them on a piece of greaseproof paper to set.

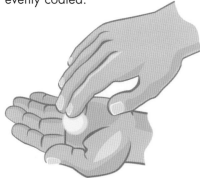

# Holiday Honeycomb

Coat honeycomb in melted chocolate or just eat it as it is!

# Holiday Honeycomb

**You will need:**

Extra equipment:
a square baking tin 18 cm (7 in.)

Ingredients:
a little butter
5 tablespoons caster sugar
2 tablespoons golden syrup
1 teaspoon bicarbonate of soda

For chocolate honeycomb:
50 g (2 oz) milk chocolate, melted

**Warning!** The honeycomb mixture will be extremely hot!

**1** Use a paper towel to grease the baking tin with a little butter. Ask an adult to help you put the sugar and syrup into a saucepan over a medium heat. Bring the mixture to the boil, then let it simmer for about 3–4 minutes until it becomes golden brown.

**2** Take the pan off the heat, add the bicarbonate of soda and mix it in with a wooden spoon. When the mixture froths up, pour it into the baking tin right away.

**3** When the mixture has cooled, turn it out onto a chopping board and use the wooden spoon to crack it into bite-size pieces.

**4** You can dip pieces of honeycomb into melted chocolate if you like! Leave to them cool on a piece of greaseproof paper.

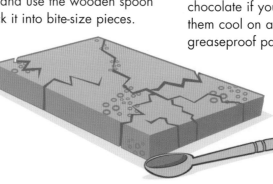

# Christmas Crunch

This crunchy treat is great to take on an outing!

# Christmas Crunch

**1** Use a paper towel to grease the tin with a little butter. Put some water in a saucepan and warm it over a low heat. Put the butter, chocolate and golden syrup into a heatproof bowl. Ask an adult to help you stand the bowl over the pan, stirring the ingredients until they have melted.

**You will need:**

Extra equipment:
a square tin 18 cm (7 in.)
a clean plastic bag
a rolling pin

**Ingredients:**
75 g (3 oz) butter
75 g (3 oz) plain chocolate
2 tablespoons golden syrup
175 g (6 oz) digestive biscuits
75 g (3 oz) raisins
25 g (1 oz) desiccated coconut
50 g (2 oz) chopped nuts

**To decorate:**
25 g (1 oz) plain chocolate
coloured chocolate drops

**Top Tip**
Dip a spoon in hot water before measuring the syrup – the heat makes the syrup slide off the spoon!

**2** Put the biscuits into a clean plastic bag and crush them with a rolling pin.

**3** Take the bowl off the pan, and add the biscuits, raisins, coconut and chopped nuts, mixing everything together thoroughly. Put the mixture into the tin, pressing it down firmly.

**4** To decorate, melt the chocolate in a clean bowl over a pan of simmering water, as before. Spread the chocolate evenly over the mixture in the tin. Mark nine squares in the chocolate crunch, and then put the chocolate drops on top. Leave it to set in a cool place for 2–3 hours and then cut it into squares.

# Christmas Toffee Pudding

Try this sticky dessert instead of traditional Christmas Pudding

# Christmas Toffee Pudding

## To make the pudding:

**1** Soak the dates in boiling water, allow to cool. Add bicarbonate of soda and mix in a food processor.

**2** Cream the butter and sugar together and beat in the egg. Carefully fold in both flours and mix in the cooled date mixture to form a sloppy dough.

**3** Pour the mixture into a medium well-buttered pudding basin and cover the top with silver foil, seal the edges and place in a preheated oven for approximately 30–40 minutes or until firm to the touch.

## You will need:

**Extra equipment:**
a heatproof pudding basin

**Ingredients:**
For the pudding:
90 g (3 oz) dried dates (stones removed)
100 ml (1/5 pt.) boiling water
1/2 tsp bicarbonate of soda
45 g (1 1/2 oz) unsalted butter
75 g (2 1/2 oz) caster sugar
1 medium egg
45 g (1 1/2 oz) plain flour
45 g (1 1/2 oz) self-raising flour
For the toffee sauce:
105 g (3 1/2 oz) demerara sugar
60 g (2 oz) butter
75 ml (2 1/2 fl oz) double cream
vanilla essence

Preheat the oven to 185°C / 360°F / gas mark 4

## To make the toffee sauce:

**1** Mix all the ingredients together in a small thick-bottomed saucepan and heat until simmering.

**2** Cook until toffee-coloured.

**Warning!**
The toffee sauce mixture will be extremely hot!

## To serve:

**1** Tip the pudding into a deep-sided, heatproof dish and pour over the hot toffee sauce.

**2** Place the dish under a hot grill for a few seconds to allow the toffee sauce to bubble.

**3** Serve with double cream or vanilla ice cream.

# Festive Fritters

These tasty little nibbles are sure to make your party go with a swing!

# Festive Fritters

## Take Note!
Ask an adult to help you use the deep fat frier.

**You will need:**
Extra equipment:
a sauce boat
a deep fat fryer

**Ingredients:**
120 g (4 oz) flour
150 ml (5 fl oz) milk
30 ml (1 fl oz) oil
1 pinch of salt
30 ml (1 fl oz) egg white
from approx. 2 eggs

**For the apricot sauce:**
16 tinned apricot halves in natural juice
60 g (2 oz) icing sugar
small jar of apricot jam

*Preheat the fryer to 180°C / 355°F*

## To make the batter:

**1** Sieve the flour into a bowl. Gradually beat in the milk to produce a smooth batter.

**2** Stir in the oil and the salt.

**3** Cover with cling film and allow the mixture to rest for at least 10 minutes.

**4** When you are ready to start cooking, beat the egg white until stiff and gently fold it into the batter.

## To cook:

**1** Pre-heat the deep fat fryer to approximately 180°C/355°F.

**2** Dust the apricot halves with a little flour and dip them into the batter.

**3** Lift them out with a fork and carefully place in the hot fat. Fry gently until the batter is golden and crisp. Lift out onto paper to drain.

**4** Dust with icing sugar and serve with hot apricot sauce, made by boiling the apricot jam with a little of the fruit juice and straining into a sauce boat.

# Christmas Caramel

A lightweight treat to follow Christmas dinner!

# Christmas Caramel

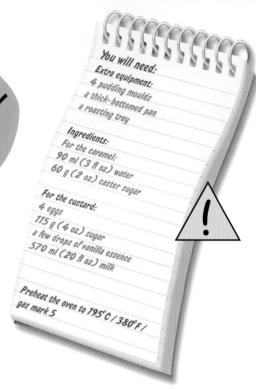

**Take Note!**
Ask an adult to help you with this recipe.

*You will need:*

**Extra equipment:**
4 pudding moulds
a thick-bottomed pan
a roasting tray

**Ingredients:**
For the caramel:
90 ml (3 fl oz) water
60 g (2 oz) caster sugar

For the custard:
4 eggs
115 g (4 oz) sugar
a few drops of vanilla essence
570 ml (20 fl oz) milk

Preheat the oven to 195°C / 380°F /
gas mark 5

## To make the caramel:

**1** Lightly grease four individual pudding moulds or soufflé dishes.

**2** Ask an adult to help you with this recipe. Make the caramel by boiling the sugar with 60 ml (2 fl oz) of the water in a thick-bottomed pan. Carefully cook until the sugar turns a golden amber colour. Remove from heat and add the last 30 ml (1 fl oz) of the water (beware of steam!).

**3** Return the pan to the heat and reboil while stirring. Divide the caramel between the four moulds. Allow to stand and form a skin.

## To make the custard:

**1** Whisk the eggs with the sugar and vanilla essence and add the milk. Strain through a fine strainer onto the caramel.

**2** Stand the moulds in a roasting tray and surround with water. Cook in a preheated oven for 30–40 minutes or until set.

**3** Allow to cool, and then thoroughly chill in a refrigerator.

**4** To serve, loosen the edges of the mould with a sharp knife and up-end on to a plate. Tap to unmould then pour the caramel over the top to surround the dish.

# Santa Snaps

A crunchy Christmas classic and one of Santa's favourites!

# Santa Snaps

**1** Melt the butter, sugar and syrup in a small pan. Stir in the flour and ginger, add the grated rind of the half lemon and 1 tablespoon of the juice.

You will need:
Extra equipment:
a baking tray
greaseproof paper

Ingredients:
60 g (2 oz) butter
60 g (2 oz) caster sugar
60 g (2 oz) golden syrup
60 g (2 oz) flour
1/2 teaspoon ground ginger
half a lemon
For the filling:
300 ml (1/2 pt) double cream
15 g (1/2 oz) icing sugar
240 g (8 1/2 oz) fresh fruit

Preheat the oven to 180°C / 350°F / gas mark 4

**Take Note!**
Graters are sharp. Ask an adult to help you.

**2** Place twelve tablespoons of the mixture well spaced on greaseproof paper and press them out. Bake them for 8–10 minutes until golden. Allow to cool slightly, and then slide off the paper onto a wire rack.

**4** Spoon fresh cream into the middle of one snap, surround with fresh fruit and sandwich with a second snap. Repeat with a third, and decorate the top with cream and fruit.

**3** Whip the cream with the icing sugar until it forms soft peaks.

**5** Repeat the process to produce three more Santa Snaps.

# Mincemeat Parcels

Try this party version of the traditional treat – delicious dipped in cream!

# Mincemeat Parcels

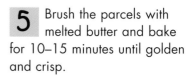

**Take Note!**
Take Note!
Ask an adult to help
you melt the butter.

**1** Take one sheet of filo pastry and brush with a little melted butter. Fold in half to sandwich the butter, cut this folded sheet in half, and again to form four equal quarters. Carefully butter the top of one quarter.

**2** Place a second quarter on top at a slight angle, butter this and repeat the process with a third and fourth square – you should have a filo star shape.

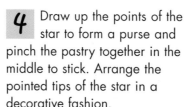

**3** Place a spoonful of mincemeat in the centre, brush round the mincemeat with egg yolk whisked with a little water.

**4** Draw up the points of the star to form a purse and pinch the pastry together in the middle to stick. Arrange the pointed tips of the star in a decorative fashion.

Use the picture on page 87 as a guide to the final shape you need to achieve, when shaping the pastry.

**5** Brush the parcels with melted butter and bake for 10–15 minutes until golden and crisp.

**6** Allow to cool slightly before serving. For a more festive look dust them with icing sugar and serve with double cream or vanilla ice cream.

# Mince Pies

Christmas wouldn't be complete without a hot mince pie!

# Mince Pies

**1** Cut the butter into cubes. Sieve the flour into a mixing bowl. Add the butter and, using your fingertips, rub the butter into the flour until it resembles fine breadcrumbs.

**Top Tip**
To soften the butter, take it out of the fridge at least 30 minutes before cooking.

You will need:
Extra equipment:
    a bun tin
    a pastry cutter

Ingredients:
200g (8 oz) butter, softened
450g (1 lb) all purpose flour
50g (2 oz) icing sugar
2 egg yolks
a cup of iced water
450g (1 lb) mincemeat
beaten egg, to glaze

Preheat the oven to 200°C / 400°F / gas mark 6

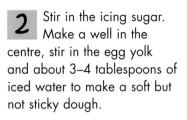

**2** Stir in the icing sugar. Make a well in the centre, stir in the egg yolk and about 3–4 tablespoons of iced water to make a soft but not sticky dough.

**3** Knead lightly to form a smooth dough and chill for 30 minutes.

**4** On a floured surface, roll out two thirds of the dough and cut out 30 rounds using the pastry cutter. Use these to line the bun tin. Fill with mincemeat.

**5** Re-roll the remaining pastry and trimmings and cut out circles using a cutter. Dampen the edges of each circle and place onto the pies.

**6** Seal the edges, brush the tops with beaten egg and cook for about 20 minutes or until they are golden brown. Ask an adult to take the hot tray from the oven. Use a spatula to transfer the mince pies to a wire rack to cool.

# Recipes

Use these pages to write down your own recipes!

# Recipes

# Recipes

# Recipes

# Recipes

# Recipes